Coloring Book

I Love Mermaids

Illustrated by

Jen Racine

instagram: @jenracinecoloring

facebook.com/jenracinecoloring

www.jenracine.com

Jen Racine Coloring Books

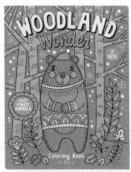   

  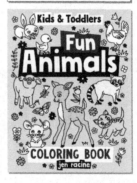 

Coloring pages in Etsy Shop:

www.etsy.com/shop/JenRacineColoring

Copyright © 2018 by Eclectic Esquire Media LLC

ISBN-13: 978-1724794031
ISBN-10: 1724794035

Made in United States
Orlando, FL
27 March 2023

31477093R00057